Sky Trucks

Sky Trucks

KARL-HEINZ MORAWIETZ
& JÖRG WEIER

OSPREY
AEROSPACE

Published in 1990 by Osprey Publishing Limited
59 Grosvenor Street, London W1X 9DA

British Library Cataloguing in Publication Data

Morawietz, Karl-Heinz
    Sky trucks.
    1. Propellor-driven planes.
    Commercial history
    I. Title   II. Weier, Jörg
    629.133343

ISBN 0 85045 9893

Editor Dennis Baldry

Captions Mike Jerram & Jörg Weier
Page design Karl-Heinz Morawietz
Printed in Hong Kong

Front cover Carga Aéro Nacionale's
DC-6 at La Paz, Bolivia, before
departing for a cattle farm deep in the
interior. This trusty Douglas is also
pictured on pages 84–87

Back cover Whenever a Santa Rita
flying meat wagon arrives at La Paz,
packers climb aboard immediately to
rush the carcasses onto a truck.
There's no refrigeration, and the meat
must arrive at market as fresh as
possible. Here C-46 Commando
CP-754 offloads after a trip to a cattle
farm in the Bolivian lowlands

Title page El Dorado's splendid
C-46 CP-1617 is also featured on
pages 100–104

'Gear up, positive rate of climb': Aero
Minas' C-46 leaves Cochabamba
bound for various destinations in
Beni, Bolivia

For a catalogue of all books published by Osprey Aerospace
please write to:

**The Marketing Manager, Consumer Catalogue Department
Osprey Publishing Ltd, 59 Grosvenor Street, London, W1X 9DA**

Introduction

Long-time collectors of the Osprey Colour Series will notice that the title of this book is a pluralized version of Stephen Piercey's classic *Sky Truck*, first published shortly after he was tragically killed as a result of a mid-air collision in April 1984. His remarkable book, together with the posthumous *Sky Truck 2*, spawned a string of related titles: *Big Props*, *Fire Bombers*, *Alaskan Props*, *Miami Props* and *Caribbean Props*. *Sky Trucks USA* is scheduled for publication in the summer of 1991.

Karl-Heinz Morawietz and Jörg Weier grew up close to Düsseldorf Airport in West Germany and became aviation enthusiasts with a special affection for piston-engined airliners. Dwindling numbers of these veteran load-haulers in European skies

encouraged them to search further afield for their favourite aircraft. Their first book in the Osprey Colour Series was *Alaskan Props*.

Sky Trucks is the first book in this 'series within a series' to be totally devoted to the ancient pelicans of Latin and Central America, the authors having revisited the airports and grass strips from which Stephen Piercey blazed his legendary trail. But it still wasn't easy: your faithful correspondents were once held at gunpoint for unwittingly trying to photograph a drug laden C-46 Commando in Columbia, and several flights were completed on the proverbial 'wing and a prayer'. The vast majority of the photographs in *Sky Trucks* were taken during 1988–89.

Contents

Not a camouflaged Dakota, but El Venado's HK-1315, still wearing the old green livery of La Urraca

Hispaniola Island

Left Typically congested ramp scene at Santo Domingo during 1988 with (left to right) Douglas DC-6, Lockheed L1049 Super Constellation, Curtiss C-46 and Boeing C-97G Stratofreighter awaiting onward loads

Below Parking attendants. None of that 'cleared to push back' stuff on Santo Domingo's crowded freight ramp. Instead, Transporte Aéreo Dominicana SA (TRADO) ground staff gather to confirm that the wingtip of Aerolineas Mundo's departing Super Connie will safely clear their bare metal DC-6

Overleaf Miami bound at 8000 feet and 210 knots, AMSA's flagship HI-515 cruises against a spectacular Caribbean sunset

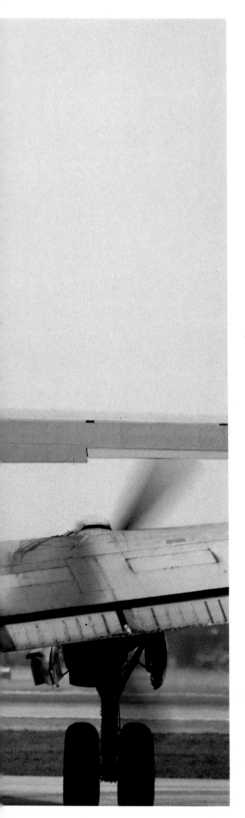

Left Quick turnarounds are SOP for these workaholic tramp steamers of the skies. After a brief night stop, HI-515 has been loaded with yet another cargo and taxies from Miami International en route to Providenciales in the Turks and Caicos islands

Above No, it is not all blue skies even here in paradise. On final descent into Providenciales some hefty thunderstorms intervened, preventing the favoured straight-in approach. HI-515's crew skirted around some massive cunim build-ups to break out on short final

This page Freight doors agape the Super Constellation rests after flying the day's first sector while ground staff unload the cargo with the aid of JCB and extending ladder

Opposite Time for reflection. HI-515 pauses in front of Providenciales' hi-tech control tower. And back home at Santo Domingo, Captain Luis Amador, his brother and co-pilot Angel, and the rest of the Super Connie's crew take a bow for the cameras of their grateful passengers

Above *Chirp, chirp.* Puffs of rubber smoke signal the arrival at San Juan, Puerto Rico, of another member of Dominica's Connie family, Aerochago SA's delectable L749 HI-422

Right With its four 2500 hp Wright 794C-18BD-1 engines thundering away, HI-422 climbs away from San Juan's Luis Munoz International Airport and sweeps into a left turn on course for home at Santo Domingo. Alas Aerochago's beautiful workhorse was written off in 1988 after damaging a nosewheel and overstressing the fuselage during the ensuing ground roll

Above and right The only replacement for a Constellation is . . . a Super Constellation. HI-228, an early model L1049 seen here in 1985, was one of three Super Connies operated by Aerochago. Today, cannibalized to support her L1049F sister ships, she rots away at Santo Domingo

Dominicana's Douglas C-118A Liftmaster HI-292, seen here at San Juan in 1985, was also kept airworthy with vital organs transplanted from the carrier's DC-6B HI-92

Opposite page Argo SA's once familiar L749 Constellation HI-328 seen at Miami prior to a much-publicized fatal crash that might have marked the end of the Connie era at the airport. But thanks to AMSA and Aerochago, Miami enthusiasts can still enjoy the elegant sight and reverberating sound of the big Lockheed classic. HI-328 was formerly United States Air Force C-121A 48-615, and once bore the name *Dewdrop* as the personal VIP transport of General Vandenburg

Below and right Gleaming in the San Juan sunshine, Air Haiti's pristine Super Commando HH-AHA *Pearl of the Antilles* takes on Avgas 100 over the wing and freight from a forklift, ready for the return trip to Port-au-Prince. Air Haiti was formed in 1969 to operate non-scheduled cargo services with C-46s and DC-6s

Another Caribbean Commando, HI-503 of the Dominican carrier Air Mar
Freight Systems, taxying to the holding point at San Juan bound for home base
at Santo Domingo

Left and above Trust in God and Pratt & Whitney. And indeed HI-503's trusty R-2800s perform as advertised, with not a hint of 'automatic rough' over the blue waters of the Caribbean. A healthy crosswind has the C-46 crabbing towards the Santo Domingo runway centreline at Santo Domingo

Buffed to distraction, with a lustre appropriate to its operator's title, Haitian Douglas DC-3 HH-EBA rests at Port-au-Prince after operating passenger flights between the Haitian capital and Santo Domingo

Another member of the mirror-bright brigade is this ex-USAF Boeing C-97G Stratofreighter which Dominican cargo hauler Agro Air put into service in 1985

First smoke of the day. The first officer checks anxiously for signs of the conflagratory pyrotechnics for which the Stratofreighter's 28-cylinder 3500 hp Pratt & Whitney R-4360 Double Wasp engines were legendary as HI-473 prepares for another trip. Agro Air's two appropriately blue-finned 'Whales' fly several times a week from Santo Domingo to such destinations as Belize, Colombia and Miami

Central America

Below Commercial operators in Latin America also continue to rely on the dependable Dizzy Six. This colourful example sporting a portrait of General Manuel José Arce is a DC-6BF of Aerolineas El Salvador (AESA)

Left Cargo-carrying Lockheed L188CF Electras of Transportes Aéreos Nacionales SA of Honduras are a frequent sight at Miami International. HR-TNN is seen over the threshold of runway 09 Left. Colloquially known in its early days as 'Shelton's Barefoot Airline', TAN was founded in 1947 by American entrepreneur C N Shelton and Honduran rancher Miguel Brooks

Another military Six from Latin American is the Fuerza Aérea Guatemalteca's immaculate FAG-926. A DC-6B, it was originally built for Olympic Airways of Greece as SX-DAD *Isle of Rhodes*, and took to military uniform with the FAG's Escuadrón de Transporte at Base Aérea La Aurora International Airport, Guatemala City in 1972. Seen here at Miami in 1980, it is currently operated in civilian markings, but remains on FAG strength

Reflected in the aftermath of a rainstorm, Fuerza Aérea Salvadoreña Douglas DC-6A FAS 301 pictured at Miami in September 1987 is one of two ex-Transportes Aéreos Centro-Americanos (TACA) aircraft which have been operated by that air arm for heavy transport duties with the Escuadrilla de Transporte at Llopango, San Salvador

Venezuela

These pages Aero B Venezuela had a much shorter history. Founded in April 1978 by former military pilots, it operated a fleet of six cargo-carrying DC-6Bs until financial collapse in 1983. This well-maintained DC-6B *Tropicana* escaped storage at Caracas and was acquired by aircraft brokers Atlas Aircraft Corporation of Opa Locka, Florida

Overleaf Aeropostal's fleet of seven British-built HS.748 twin turboprops operates domestic services throughout Venezuela. YV-46C is seen here at Caracas's La Maiquetia Airport in February 1980. Aeropostal, formerly Linea Aeropostal Venezolana (LAV) was founded on 1 January 1935

Colombia

These pages and next page Colombia boasts one of South America's largest populations of piston-engined airliners. Villavicencio, in jungle territory east of the Andes, is famous for its props-only operations. It is the home of Servicios Aéreos del Vaupes Ltda which operates C-46s and DC-3s, two of which are seen here against a backdrop of the airfield's modern control tower and terminal building. Commando HK-851 has been a Colombian resident for over 30 years

Appropriately enough, SELVA is also a Spanish word for bushland or jungle.
Here SELVA's second C-46 HK-3150 leaves Villavicencio to head southeast for
Miraflores and Mitu, a 300 mile trip over dense rain forest, with tricky
approaches into short and muddy strips at the end of it. Note the air
conditioning system—crew entry door in the cargo hatch left open until the
last moment!

Two SELVA *méchanicos* probe the innards of HK-122's Twin Wasps to ensure another uneventful trip for the brightly decorated C-47-DL. Named *Miss Carriage*, 122 was originally delivered to the USAAF 8th Air Force in England in 1942. She first arrived in South America in 1947 for service with Aerovias Nacionales de Colombia SA (AVIANCA)

Far left 0530. Temperature 75°F. Humidity 98%. Maintenance completed, HK-122 greets the sun at the start of another busy day

Above Although SELVA is technically an 'all-freight' airline, passengers are carried if they can be squeezed in between fuel barrels and cargo crates

Left Ready for departure, but a brewing tropical storm may flood the airstrip in minutes, and throw flight plans off schedule for days

C-46 Commando HK-812 was operated by the now defunct Intercontinental Colombia when photographed in 1985, but is now operated by Aerosol (no jokes about the ozone layer, please . . .)

Wherever there's bush flying to be done, be sure you'll find de Havilland
Canada's sturdy DHC-2 Beaver. This smartly painted example is part of the
Vias Aéreas Colombianas (VIARCO) fleet, and is one of many Beavers which
have done sterling service in Colombia's rugged terrain

C-47 HK-337 of ARCA Colombia at Villavicencio in 1980, two years before it
was written off in a landing collision at Pacon with HK-124 of LACOL

Right Taxi Aereo El Venado (Spanish for deer) at one time operated eight DC-
3s/C-47s, three DC-4s, two Beech Queen Airs and a Britten-Norman Islander.
Undergoing maintenance in the rain at Mitu, this C-47 (HK-140), is an ex-
AVIANCA aircraft, having previously served with VARIG in Brazil after
demob from the USAAF

Preceding spread and above Landing light on and rudder and tailwheel at full left deflection, Transamazonica Ltda's HK-1175 edges out from a tight parking space at Villavicencio as its co-pilot checks clearance with a Cessna 172 before the Dak thunders down the field's single runway. HK-1175's colour scheme suggests a former career as a corporate transport

Top right El Dorado's business rival Servicio Aerea del Caqueta (SADELCA) doubled its fleet of DC-3s in 1987 by taking over El Dorado's two aircraft. Here one of the original pair, HK-1338, takes on fuel at Villavicencio

Bottom right Lineas Aéreas El Dorado Ltda's spotless C-47A-60-DL HK-2666 takes aboard groceries and other essentials. Like most second level operators, El Dorado played a vital role in maintaining lifelines to Colombia's underdeveloped regions in the southeast of the country, HK-2666 previously served with the USAAF, Royal Canadian Force, the Muscat & Oman Air Force, and commercial carriers in Norway and Canada before joining El Dorado in 1981

Now an all-jet carrier equipped with Boeing 707s, TAMPA was once proud operator of two well-travelled DC-6s. HK-1776 *Luis H Coulson* awaits some action on the ramp at Bogota in 1980

The DC-7B is a rare sight even in Latin America. During the early 1980s the Fuerza Aérea Colombiana's Comando Aéreo de Transporte Militar operated this sole example, FAC-921. Its origin is a mystery, though the faded Zantop Airlines insignia on the fuselage suggests to the authors that it may have been the former N751Z, c/n 44923, which was once American Airlines' N387AA

Colombia's paramilitary airline SATENA (Servicio de Aeronavegación a Territorios Nacionales) was founded in September 1962, and is operated by the Fuerza Aérea Colombiana. Its purpose is to maintain 'social service' air links with isolated territories and scattered settlements which no unsubsidized commercial operator would serve. From the looks of the baggage carts and boarding queue, SATENA's morning service from Bogota to Puerto Asis was fully booked on 9 April 1985 when C-54 Skymaster FAC 695 was operating the flight

Right and following page After counting the ritual twelve blades go by, FAC-695's crew fire up number three, and with all four turning, head for the holding point at Bogota

On top, en route. FAC-695's number three and four engines seen through the scratched and oil-stained plexiglass of the Skymaster's distinctive porthole windows

Below A surprise visitor to Miami in late 1987 was this freshly painted C-118 Liftmaster HK-1702 of Lineas Aereas del Caribe. The company usually operates Boeing 707s, but presses this grand old stager into service when the upstart young jets go unserviceable

Right All temperatures and pressures in the green, flaps set 20 degrees, landing lights on, HK-1702 is ready to roll for the eight hour trip to Colombia

Aerolineas Nacionales del Ecuador SA, whose title forms the appropriate acronym ANDES, was founded in 1961 by Capitano Alfredo V Franco del Monaco and is one of few Latin American cargo carriers to hold a US Civil Aeronautics Board all-freight certificate. DC-6A HC-AQB joined the ANDES fleet in 1968 and is seen here at her home base at Guayaquil after a short flight from the nation's capital Quito. The DC-6A was later replaced with a DC-8-33F

Ecuador

ANDES' Canadair CL-44-6 HC-AZH was a former Canadian Armed Forces CC-106 Yukon and lacks the 'swing tail' of commercial CL-44 variants. After leaving CAF service HC-AZH flew as CF-JSN with Beaver Enterprises before joining the Ecuadorean carrier's fleet. It is seen here in 1980 ready for departure from Miami International bound for Ecuador via Panama

End of the line. Once the pride of SARCO's small fleet in the 1970s, DC-3 HC-AYB seems to have lost the struggle for survival, and rots sadly in the graveyard at Quito

Servicios Aéreos Nacionales' Vickers Viscount 828 HC-ATV, seen here on
finals to Quito, was the last but one Viscount built, and served previously with
All Nippon Airways of Japan. SAN began scheduled services in October 1967.
Its route between Quito and Quiyaquil is one of the most frequent and efficient
inter-city services in Latin America

Right and preceding spread Like many Latin American nations, Ecuador has a government-subsidized airline. Transportes Aéreos Militares Ecuatorianas (TAME) has been operated by the Fuerza Aérea Ecuatoriana since 1963 and in its early years played a key role in developing air services to the Galapágos Islands. Seen here at Guayaquil in TAME's attractive old colour scheme are Lockheed L188A Electra HC-AZL/FAE-1050 *Guayas* and L188C HC-AZJ/FAE-2004 *Pichincha*, wearing dual civil registrations/military serial numbers. The Electra era finally came to an end in September 1989 when HC-AZJ, then the last flying example on the TAME fleet, suffered a landing gear malfunction while en route from Quito to Quiyaquil and was forced to belly-land at Taura Air Force Base. The beautiful turboprop airliner was damaged beyond economical repair

Below The FAE's Grupo de Transportes Aéreos Militares 11 at Mariscal Sucre International Airport, Quito, operates a fleet of four Hawker Siddeley HS.748s, one Presidential aircraft and three which support TAME services. This camouflaged example is an HS.748–285 HC-BAZ/FAE-738. Note the inscription on the nosewheel door: *Avro 748 Equipado con Radar*. In an age when few commerical aircraft are *not* equipped with weather radar, this confidence-boosting boast from the 1950s is still to be found on some South American transports, whose owners don't hesitate to turn now-standard features into a bonus! Most of the FAE/TAME C-47s in the background have now been retired

Bolivia

Bolivia's rugged terrain seen from a Lloyd Aereo Boliviano Boeing 727 approaching the capital La Paz on a flight from Lima, Peru. Though officially called Aeropuerto Internacional J F Kennedy, La Paz's airport is also known as *Aeropuerto El Alto* – the high one. With good reason. At 13,358 feet above sea level it is the highest commerical airport in the world

Opposite page This is my world. The two American sub-continents decorate the nose of this Curtiss C-46 Commando, which saw previous service in the United States, India, Sweden, Colombia and Brazil

Weather at La Paz is capricious. Within minutes the 18,000 foot peaks behind
Universal's CP-1655 had disappeared completely in cloud

Paved taxiways are a luxury in Bolivia

Left You don't get sparkling performance at these rarified altitudes. Fifteen minutes after take-off the Commando is still circling to gain sufficient altitude for safe passage through the mountains. The C-46 is an old campaigner when it comes to mountain flying. After an inauspicious start in USAAF service the Commando became the Hero of the Hump during WW2, flying over the Himalayas on the China Airlift

Above An anonymous meat-hauling C-46, CP-746, returns to La Paz after night-stopping at a remote cattle farm at San Ramon in the province of Beni

Several Martin 4-0-4 airliners found their way to Bolivia, but only CP-1738 *El Gordo* survived. Maintenance, Bolivian style, continued for days on the 4-0-4's starboard P&W R-2800

These and following pages The C-46 is still the most widely used aircraft in
Bolivia, but the Convairliner has become a popular alternative. SASA's tired
looking CV-440 returns to her hardstanding with the No 1 engine misfiring and
trailing smoke. Transportes Aéreos America's Metropolitan CP-1574 once
carried holidaymakers to Florida and the Bahamas in Mackey International
colours. Now she hauls freshly slaughtered meat to La Paz from the tropical
farms in the north east of Bolivia

Tired Iron. A dismembered C-46 rests at *El Alto*. But who can be sure that it may not fly again one day?

These pages and preceding spread Deep maintenance in the open is *de rigueur* in Bolivia. Within 24 hours Carga Aéro Nacionale's DC-6 CP-1654 had been fired up and was on her way to La India, a cattle farm on the other side of the Andes. CP-1654 is one of the oldest surviving Sixes, delivered new to American Airlines in 1947 as N90730, *Flagship El Paso*. Heavy rain was forecast at her destination but the crew elected to go just the same. Next morning we learned that the DC-6 was unable to return to La Paz—stuck axle-deep in mud at La India

After a period of inactivity Bolivan carrier La Cumbre is in action again with DC-6A CP-1282, first operated by Loide Aéreo Nacional of Brazil. Not for nothing is La Paz's runway 09R/27L 4000 metres long. At these rarified altitudes engine performance is dramatically reduced, and sometimes every inch of tarmac is needed to get airborne

Frigorifico Santa Rita, a La Paz-based meat trader, could not resist adding four-engines to its small fleet. But this former TAXPA-Chile DC-6's 12-ton cargo capacity could not be economically employed, and it remains grounded at *El Alto*

Frig Santa Rita's venerable C-47 CP-529 may be weathered, but it is still going
strong after 45 years in Bolivian skies

Taking the bull by the tail: Frig Santa Rita's DC-6, C-47 and C-46 at La Paz

Left and above Sunlight catches the propeller blades of ageing and timeworn Convair C-131B CP-1676 as the crew release brakes, ease forward on the throttles and rumble away to *El Alto's* holding point

These pages and overleaf Frigerificos Reyes was once the largest freight operator in Bolivia. At its height Fri Reyes flew a dozen heavy piston types, including the celebrated B-17 Flying Fortresses. Business slumped in 1988 and during our visit the Fri Reyes ramp at La Paz resembled a graveyard. Despite being *equipado con radar* the DC-6 shows no signs of getting back into the air, while DC-4 CP-1653 bears witness to a post-take-off engine fire which severely damaged the port wing and fuselage

Opposite page When in La Paz, ask for Victor Cabrera. For a few *Dollares* this kindly taxi driver provides transportation to downtown La Paz and all parts of *El Alto*— on time, safely and in reliable Japanese equipment!

Left Every meat hauler has its own troop of guard dogs. This pair of mongrels look after El Dorado Ltda's C-46 Super Commando CP-1617, and for their labours enjoy a juicy portion of the cargo, seen being offloaded by that most reliable of freight handling systems, a strong back

Left and above Before each flight CP-1617's Twin Wasps undergo a 20-minute run-up to ensure that all systems are working perfectly. An engine failure in the mountainous terrain around La Paz is almost certain death. When these pictures were taken on 27 January 1989 bad weather had delayed *El Mestizo's* departure for two days until the crew saw a chance of crossing the Andes for the one and a half hour flight to the hacienda of Palmira

Four crew, two avid sky truckers from Germany, a local passenger and four tons of blood-dripping meat, including this unhappy pig, made up the Commando's load this day

It may look like waste, but this will feed an Indio family for days. Low incomes from flying force the meat hauling crews to trade in meat on their own account, and with meat prices in La Paz running at five times those in Beni, it is worth the trouble

Left No view from the greenhouse. On the return leg to La Paz we encountered solid IFR weather with zero visibility, airframe ice and turbulence—hardly the best conditions for threading a heavily-laden C-46 through a narrow pass in the Andes. Airspeed is 160 mph, altitude just over 6800 feet. At 18,000 feet an oxygen cylinder was passed back and forth among the unpressurized Commando's occupants

Above All in a day's work for them: safely back at La Paz, C-46 skipper Walter Ballivan and co-pilot Walter Ballivan Jnr

Right and main picture Curtiss C-46 CP-900 of Servicios Aéreos Bolivianos is in open store at Cochabamba, home to some colourful operators of piston engined airliners. Odd that no-one thought to decorate that inviting yellow snout, or hasn't the Smiley button reached Bolivia?

Below Serious maintenance on a Trans Aéreo Virgen del Carmen C-46 at Aeropuerto Jorge Wilstermann, Cochabamba

Left and above Rush hour, Cochabamba style. In 30 minutes no fewer than five heavy piston types launched from the runway bound for destinations in Beni. What a sight! What a sound! The very stuff to get an enthusiast's heart pumping faster. This Aéro Minas C-46 CP-987 was followed by Dakota CP-1622 of Trans Aéreos Cochabamba

DC-3-201 CP-1128 of Trans Aéreos San Miguel takes a well-earned rest at
Cochabamba. Originally NC18122 of the Eastern Airlines 'Great Silver Fleet'
after delivery in November 1937, this DC-3 was impressed into USAAF service
as a C-49G, returned to Eastern after WW2 and had a lengthy career as a
corporate transport in the USA before sale to Bolivia in 1974. At some stage it
has had a cargo door added

Overleaf Curtiss deep, mountain high. Can you spot the C-46 in the Cochabamba circuit?

This page A new addition to the Bolivian DC-3 inventory is this aircraft of Trans Aéreos San Antonio, whose colour scheme betrays previous service with the US Federal Aviation Administration

Top left and above NEBA's CP-1616 is one of the smartest Commandos in service. The heady smells of Avgas, hot oil and freshly slaughtered meat attend its arrival

Below left Gear down and locked, landing flap set, North East Bolivian Airways' C-46 CP-1616 turns from base leg onto final approach for Cochabamba's Runway 04. The cracks in the windscreen? Par for the course and nothing to worry about

This page and opposite NEBA's other aircraft is Convair CV-440 CP-1040, but despite full company livery it appears to be inactive, unlike the hard working Commando. Let's hope NEBA will continue to find enough work and spare parts to keep 'Old Dumbo' flying into the next century

Bottom right *El Commandante* Flores (left) and *Primer Official* Zigarra, two typical *carniceros*, as the meat flyers are known in Bolivia

Interesting (terrifying?) final approach paths are common in South America. Here a Lloyd Aéreo Boliviano Boeing 727 heads for touchdown at Cochabamba against a mountain backdrop, to make an intermediate stop en route from La Paz to Santa Cruz

Brazil

After a very brief USAF career and a short spell with the Hughes Tool Company, C-47A-50-DL PP-VBF joined the Brazilian carrier VARIG in December 1947 and operated with the line until 1971. Since then it has been the main attraction for children in Rio's Parque do Flamengo

Top left Cruzeiro Aerofoto's survey equipped C-47 PT-AOB photographed at
Rio de Janeiro's Santos Dumont Airport in October 1979

Bottom left Campo dos Alfonsos, in a suburb of Rio, is well known to
enthusiasts as the home of the excellent Museu Aerospacial da Forca Aérea
Brasileira. It also accommodated a dozen DC-3s in 1980, including this former
Viacao Aérea São Paulo (VASP) machine PT-KUD

Above The *Clube Nautico Agua Limpa* (Aquatic Sports Club, Clean Water)
maintained a fleet of four DC-3s in the late 1970s, but none of them were float-
equipped . . .

Right In Brazil 'airline' means VARIG, and for propeller fans, VARIG is synonymous with the Lockheed Electra. Introduced in 1975 on the airline's *Ponte Aérea* (air bridge) link between the downtown Rio-Santos Dumont Airport (where jets had been banned) and São Paulo-Congonhas, VARIG's dozen-strong fleet of Electras operated half-hourly no-reservations airbus services between the two cities, averaging 37 round trips each weekday, 22 at weekends. PP-VLX is an L188A, formerly operated by American Airlines as N6116A

Last page Twin jets and two-man flight decks? Forget 'em. Four props and three crew are the only way to go